Anxiety

and Panic

Attacks

Jordan Lee

THE ROSEN PUBLISHING GROUP, INC./NEW YORK

Published in 1997 by The Rosen Publishing Group, Inc.
29 East 21st Street, New York, NY 10010

First Edition

Cover photo by Olga Vega

Library of Congress Cataloging-in-Publication Data

Lee, Jordan.
    Coping with anxiety and panic attacks / Jordan Lee.
        p.   cm. — (Coping)
    Includes bibliographical references and index.
    ISBN 0-8239-2548-X (lib. bdg.)
    1. Anxiety.   2. Anxiety in adolescence.   I. Title.   II. Series.
RC531.L345   1997
616.85'223—dc21   97-14367
                                                                   CIP
                                                                   AC

Manufactured in the United States of America

ABOUT THE AUTHOR ◇

Jordan Lee is a psychotherapist and lecturer practicing in Tulsa, Oklahoma. She is one of the coordinators for Anxiety Screening Day in Tulsa.

She is also a freelance writer and has written numerous self-help books for teens.

Contents

Introduction

One afternoon as I was walking home from high school, I realized that I was being followed. A car had been slowly moving along behind me, and when I'd look around, the driver would speed up and pass me, only to slow down again. As I neared my neighborhood, I decided to take a shortcut. But as I scurried down a side street, I saw the car parked at the end of the street. Panic seized me. Someone was waiting for me at the end of the street. My heart started pounding, my insides turned to ice, and I turned around and ran for the nearest convenience store. I've never run so fast.

In this case, panic served me well. Faced with certain danger, my body reacted in the age-old fight or flight response, enabling me to escape. My heart sped up; blood was diverted to my legs so I could run faster, and I breathed harder to get more oxygen. The panic reaction *when faced with danger* is a normal, adaptive reaction. It puts you in a better position to flee danger or turn to fight it.

Sometimes, however, symptoms of anxiety or panic occur when there is no visible threat. Some people feel just the way I felt when that man was following me, except that they are merely walking into a grocery store.

Clearly, something is wrong when anxiety and panic kick in and no danger is present. It is no longer adaptive or normal. In fact, if you don't do something about it, you'll wear yourself out. I wrote this book because I, like

1

millions of other people, suffer from anxiety, and I've learned to manage it. You can, too. Some of you may only be very shy teenagers who panic when you're around a lot of people. Believe it or not, that's a very common social phobia that most adolescents outgrow.

There are many different types, and symptoms, of anxiety disorders. Some of you may have thoughts or actions—like washing your hands or saying certain phrases—that you feel as though you must repeat over and over to quell anxiety. Those, too, are signs of an anxiety disorder—obsessive compulsive disorder. Obsessive compulsive disorder, or OCD, frequently begins in the teenage years, although it's often not diagnosed until later.

Fear of heights, spiders, and thunderstorms can happen to teenagers and even young kids. Sometimes the fear springs from a traumatic experience; sometimes it's not related to anything at all.

This book discusses the major anxiety disorders, exploring what probably causes them and how to treat them. It looks at ordinary stress and discusses ways to avoid going from "stressed" to "anxious and panicked." If you can learn better ways to manage stress, as well as symptoms of panic and anxiety, you can overcome many of your fears and go on to lead a happy, productive life.

A LOOK AT ANXIETY AND ITS DISORDERS

CHAPTER ◇ 1

What Are Anxiety Disorders and Panic Attacks?

Anxiety comes in many forms. Aside from momentary episodes, you can have *generalized anxiety* (which seems to be a catchall term for chronic anxiety), *panic attacks with agoraphobia* (which is a more intense and crippling experience, causing avoidance of everywhere but home), and *panic attacks without agoraphobia*.

GENERALIZED ANXIETY

Anxiety causes three types of reactions: physiological (the physical sensations), cognitive (the ways people think about their situation), and behavioral (what people do about their situation).

The most common physiological sensations of generalized anxiety are gastrointestinal upsets: butterflies in the stomach, nausea, vomiting, and diarrhea. To relieve these symptoms, you may take antacids or antidiarrheal medication, especially when you face an anxiety-provoking event. Many people with these reactions end up with ulcers. Other common complaints include frequent headaches and bruxism (the clenching or grinding of teeth).

Cognitive reactions to stress—the way you think about anxiety—may make it worse. For instance, if someone is constantly worrying about getting sick to his stomach, he may actually help bring on the sickness. A person may also become very sensitive emotionally, feeling criticized, edgy, irritable, or jittery.

A person's behavior also can contribute to anxiety. Someone may avoid situations that will increase the symptoms. Another common reaction to anxiety is automatically to reach for medication without making an effort to talk yourself through the situation.

While reading this book, you may start thinking that these symptoms and reactions sound familiar. Just remember that only a trained professional such as a psychologist, clinical social worker, outpatient therapist, psychiatrist, or clincal nurse, can make a proper diagnosis of an anxiety disorder. It's important to remember that you're not alone, and that you can seek professional help if you feel you need it.

PANIC ATTACKS WITH AND WITHOUT AGORAPHOBIA

Panic is the body's way of preparing a person to flee or turn to fight when encountering a threat. Because panic attacks are so disabling to some, they may lead to agoraphobia—a fear of leaving the house. More than 2.4 million Americans suffer from panic attacks.

Fear or panic are normal reactions to danger. They set off a chain of events in the body by activating the autonomic nervous system, which controls our breathing, digestion, and temperature regulation. The autonomic nervous system is composed of two parts: the sympathetic nervous system (SNS) and the parasympathetic nervous system (PNS). The job of the SNS is to rev up a person, whereas the job of the PNS is to calm down that person afterward. The two parts balance out each other.

When you're frightened, the SNS releases adrenaline with dramatic results. Your heart pumps harder to make your blood circulate more quickly through your body to where it's most needed. You're aware only of your pounding, racing heart, or the tingling sensations in your hands and feet. What happens is that blood is diverted from the hands and feet to the larger muscles.

Your lungs get into the action, too. They work harder to draw in more air. You start to breathe harder and faster, and to sweat. The adrenaline causes you to focus more intently on the immediate danger. Your body is now totally aroused and ready to fight.

Were it not for the PNS, your body would remain aroused indefinitely, and the heightened responses would wreak havoc with your health. Thus, once the danger is past, the PNS takes over, destroying the adrenaline and bringing the body back into a relaxed state.

A panic attack occurs when the body has these heightened responses and no danger is present. Your SNS is activated, but since there is no danger to contend with, the body can't get rid of the adrenaline. Eventually, the PNS kicks in and the symptoms diminish. In the meantime, you may be left wondering if you're about to die. Since you see no visible danger, you may decide the danger is inside yourself. You may think you're having a heart attack.

Many anxious people run to the nearest emergency room, only to learn that their EKG reveals no sign of heart trouble. They're told they've had a panic attack. In an attempt to make sense out of the panic, they look for a possible cause. Once they think they've located that cause, they avoid it in the future. This avoidance may eventually lead to agoraphobia.

Agoraphobia literally means a fear of the marketplace, and it is often assumed that that means a fear of open places. Yet agoraphobics fear more than just open areas. They fear grocery stores, malls, other people's houses, church, concert halls, school, and sports arenas—just about everyplace except the safety of their own home.

For example, LaDawn Harris's mother suffered from panic attacks with agoraphobia. She rarely left the house unless she took an extra dose of her medication. Even then, she would not mingle with other people.

LaDawn once invited her mother to her soccer game. Mrs. Harris sat at the end of one of the bleachers, but people arrived late for the game and asked her to move over to make room for them on the bleacher.

When Mrs. Harris saw that she was hemmed in on all sides by people, she panicked. She felt her heart racing, and she couldn't get enough air into her lungs. The harder she breathed, the more dizzy she became. Her fingers felt tingly, and she thought, "I'm going to faint. I'm going to faint right here in front of everyone."

Sweat poured down her face, and it wasn't hot outside. LaDawn was on the field; there was no one to help her.

Mrs. Harris suddenly stood up. "I've got to get out of here," she screamed. She pushed some teenagers aside and worked her way to the side of the bleacher. "Let me by," she kept saying. Other parents were looking at her and whispering. She didn't care. She needed to get back to her car where she could breathe.

She ran the length of the field to the parking lot, searching for her car keys on the way. She unlocked the door, scrambled inside, and quickly locked the door behind her. Then she rocked back and forth until she was finally calm again. It was the last time she went to one of her daughter's soccer games.

People who have panic attacks are afraid of having further attacks. The sensation of being out of control—pounding heart, hyperventilating, sweating, and going numb—is so overwhelming that they do almost anything to avoid feeling that way again. For some, it means avoiding places that bring on attacks. For others, it means avoiding anyplace where escape is difficult. Eventually a person with agoraphobia can't leave the house unless she is with a "safe person"—someone on whom she relies to keep her calm.

The person who can't leave the safety of her home is said to be suffering from panic attacks *with* agoraphobia. The person who is still willing to go out and about is said to suffer from panic attacks *without* agoraphobia.

Nocturnal Panic Attacks

It is also possible to experience panic attacks when you sleep. My father suffered from nocturnal panic attacks. Every so often, he'd awake in the middle of the night feeling as if he were suffocating. His heart would be pounding, his pulse racing, and his fingers and toes would feel tingly and numb. Thinking he was having a heart attack, he'd jump out of bed. But after making it to the bathroom without incident, he'd realize it was one of his "spells." He'd return to bed without further trouble once the adrenaline dissipated through his body.

Nocturnal panic attacks are not uncommon. In these cases, the body's alarm is unexplicably triggered and the SNS is activated. People seem to stop having these attacks by the time they reach their sixties.

A panic attack, whether nocturnal or not, lasts only ten to twenty minutes. The symptoms gradually diminish when the PNS kicks in.

Panic and Post-Traumatic Stress Disorder

Jonathan saw both his brothers gunned down in a drive-by shooting in front of his house. Now, whenever he sees slow-moving cars driving through his neighborhood, he has a panic attack.

Rachel was sexually abused by her stepfather from the age of six until she left home at sixteen. Every night she lay in bed, dreading the sound of his footsteps coming down the hall. Now in her late teens, she can't sleep unless all the lights are on in the apartment.

Tracy witnessed a horrible car accident while she was waiting to cross the street. A truck crashed into a car waiting to make a left turn, and the car's occupant was thrown through the windshield. Now Tracy suffers from nightmares and panic attacks. She sees the body fly through the windshield over and over.

What do these three people have in common? They all suffer from post-traumatic stress disorder (PTSD). A trauma is any event outside the normal range of human experience. People who have been sexually abused, or who have witnessed natural disasters (such as tornadoes, fires, and floods), or manmade disasters (such as shootings, car accidents, and kidnappings), have all been through traumas.

People who suffer from PTSD show three major symptoms: hypervigilance (being on guard at all times), intrusion (thinking about the trauma, having nightmares), and constriction (limiting their lifestyle to avoid thinking about the trauma). The hypervigilance and intrusion lead to panic attacks, and the constriction may lead to agoraphobia as the person tries to avoid situations reminiscent of the trauma.

When people start to avoid certain situations, they're often on their way to developing phobias, which is the focus of the next chapter.

What Are Phobias and Obsessive Compulsive Disorder?

T onya was relaxing in a bubble bath. She put the book she was reading on the floormat and slid down into the warm, sudsy water. Suddenly out of the corner of her eye she saw something move. Something with long legs crawling up the cabinet, under the sink.

A spider.

Tonya bolted upright into a seated position and screamed. "Kill it; kill it!"

But no one was home.

She froze. Maybe she should leave it alone.

But then it would be there whenever she used the bathroom. Or it might crawl into her room at night.

She looked around for a weapon. Spying her shoe within arm's reach, she made a tentative move. She edged her hand toward the shoe, keeping an eye on the spider. Her heart was pounding, and even in the warm water she felt an icy coldness sweeping through her body.

Her fingers touched the shoe and pulled it toward her. Slowly, she eased herself out of the tub. Trying to decide how to approach it, she stared at the spider. Finally, she threw the shoe; the spider sped across the cabinet door and scooted inside.

Tonya screamed again. She grabbed her towel and raced out of the room. Her heart was still pounding, and she was having trouble breathing normally. She couldn't help but think the spider was plotting the quickest route to her bedroom.

The rest of the afternoon, Tonya stayed away from the bathroom. The water in the tub had grown cold. Tonya felt silly for letting a stupid little spider scare her away, but she just couldn't bring herself to go back in there. When her brother came home, she sent him in to find it and kill it.

A phobia is a strong fear of something that lasts over time. Tonya clearly was phobic about spiders. Phobias are often related to panic attacks because a person experiences the same set of symptoms when exposed to the thing he or she dreads as he or she does in a panic attack.

SIMPLE PHOBIAS

When people are afraid of specific *things*, they are said to be suffering from simple phobias. They aren't truly phobic, however, until they start avoiding, or wanting to avoid, the thing that frightens them.

People are phobic of various things. Many people are afraid of heights. My husband is afraid of heights because he fears falling. I'm also afraid of heights, but I'm afraid I'll jump. Other people are afraid of snakes, spiders, dogs, strangers, dentists and doctors, or water. Often, simple phobias result from traumatic experiences. Kids who were bitten by dogs often grow up to be phobic about dogs. People injured in car accidents are sometimes phobic about driving again. A young client of mine is phobic about water. She never swims, and she'll go for days without taking a bath or shower. One day she told me why: Her mother had tried to drown her in the bathtub when she was a little girl.

Many people are uncomfortable around certain things. This does not necessarily mean they have a phobia. I may not like the dentist, but I still go regularly. A fear is not a phobia unless you have to alter your life in order to manage the fear.

SOCIAL PHOBIAS

When I was in high school, I developed difficulty swallowing. Every time I tried to eat something, I felt as if I'd lost the ability to swallow. I just couldn't make the food go down; I gagged instead. It was particularly bad in public, so I avoided any occasions where I would have to eat in company.

On one occasion, I was asked to attend a Father/Daughter banquet with an old family friend. I thought I'd be okay because I knew this man well, and besides, the dinner was just a small part of the evening.

I was having a great time until they began to serve the food. With the very first mouthful, I couldn't swallow. My face flushed; the room was suddenly too hot, but my hands felt cold and clammy. I thought I was choking, and I gagged as I tried to force down the food.

Was everyone looking at me? My heart pounded. Could they hear it? I couldn't spit the food out; I was mortified. What if I got sick? I was breathing faster now and feeling a little dizzy. What if I passed out right here? How far away was the hospital?

Miraculously, the food finally went down. Relief swept over me and I felt my face cool down—until I scooped up the next forkful. Panic set in again. I repeated the whole procedure: try to swallow, gag, try again to swallow, gag some more, finally swallow and breathe.

The only thing I can say for the entire dinner is that I survived it, and eventually they came and took away my plate. I was quite relaxed and happy after that. However, when I was asked to my school's dinner-dance later that year, I almost refused to go; I wasn't sure I could survive another public dinner.

I had a social phobia—a fear of embarrassing myself in public. I didn't learn until many years later that this condition had a name, and that social phobias are very common with teenagers. Fear of choking is the second most common form of social phobia. The first is fear of speaking in public.

Although social phobias frequently begin in late childhood and extend into a person's early twenties, most people seem to outgrow them. I am relieved to say that I have outgrown mine.

Social phobias differ from simple phobias in that the real fear is of embarrassing yourself. People may be afraid of using the bathroom in public, eating in public, using the telephone in public, or even signing their name in public. People who suffer from social phobias typically fear being observed, thinking that others are laughing at them, or finding fault with them. So they start avoiding places where they may feel these things.

How can you tell if a person has agoraphobia or a social phobia? If the person avoids going to the mall or the grocery store because she's afraid she'll do something to embarrass herself, she has a social phobia. If the person avoids going to those same places because she's afraid she'll have a panic attack and not be able to get away, she suffers from agoraphobia.

Some people who have panic attacks develop phobias. They experience a panic attack and then try to find a logical explanation for it. If they panicked while driving down the highway, they associate the panic attack with the highway. Then they avoid driving on the highway. The avoidance reinforces the fear and contributes to the development of a phobia. If they continue to have panic attacks in other circumstances, their list of things to avoid grows. Eventually, they become housebound and agoraphobic.

OBSESSIVE COMPULSIVE DISORDER

Mike had just obtained his driver's license and was driving home from work one night. On a desolate stretch of road, he thought to himself that it was a place he'd sure hate to have a flat tire. Within minutes, he began to worry that something was wrong with his back tire. He finally pulled over and got out to check. Both back tires looked fine. As he put the car in gear again, he had the nagging suspicion that something was really wrong with the tire. He grabbed the flashlight again and took one more look at the tire.

Angry with himself, he got back into the car. "I really don't like being out here like this," he muttered.

He hadn't driven more than a quarter mile when he felt an overwhelming need to check the tire again. But this time, he wondered if the problem was really with the tire. Maybe he had run over something—or someone. He got out and examined the tires carefully. There was no sign of blood or punctures.

Still, maybe he should go back and look along the side of the road. Maybe someone was lying there right now bleeding to death.

He turned the car around and checked along the side of the road. Nothing. Once again, he started back home. A mile down the road, he again had to turn around and check "just one more time." In the end, it took him an additional hour and a half to make it home from work. Each night he worked, Mike had trouble driving home without stopping about twenty times to check whether he had driven over someone. He didn't dare tell anyone what was going on, for fear they'd think he was crazy. Then he began to wonder if indeed he *was* crazy.

Mike wasn't crazy, although he felt as if he were at the mercy of his strange compulsion to check. He had obsessive compulsive disorder. This often starts in adolescence, particularly with boys.

Obsessive compulsive disorder means having persistent, distressing thoughts, and repeating either certain behaviors (like handwashing or checking) or mental acts (like praying or counting) to cancel out these thoughts.

As you can tell from the name, obsessive compulsive disorder has two distinct parts: obsessions and compulsions. Obsessions are thoughts that won't go away. They are unwanted, uncontrollable, and often inappropriate, such as thinking you might stab someone with a knife that's left on the kitchen counter. Compulsions then develop in response to obsessions. Repeating certain physical or mental tasks over and over helps to buy some relief from the anxiety of the obsession.

Everyone has inappropriate thoughts from time to time, and everyone has routines, but someone is said to have obsessive compulsive disorder when a routine interferes with the rest of his or her life.

The most common routine is checking. Some people have to keep checking to see if they turned off the stove, turned out the lights, or locked the front door. They don't just check once or twice; they may check twenty or thirty times. Other people have compulsions to touch things, certain rituals for walking through doorways, and certain ways of getting dressed for school each day. Failing to perform their rituals brings on excruciating discomfort. Many people believe that harm will come to a loved one if they don't comply with their urges.

In fact, the fear that something bad will happen is so common in people with obsessive compulsive disorder that it is characterized as a "what if" illness. Someone may constantly worry that she will be responsible for a terrible act—poisoning a friend or pushing her mother down a flight of stairs. Also, the nature of the obsessions and compulsions can be related. Someone who constantly fears doing something blasphemous may pray compulsively; someone who is obsessed about contamination may compulsively wash his hands.

ORDINARY ANXIETY

All people feel anxiety at some time. That's normal. A shy teenager who doesn't want to give a speech in class doesn't necessarily have a social phobia. The little boy who worries endlessly that his father is going to die during open-heart surgery doesn't necessarily have obsessive compulsive disorder.

In the face of danger, the panic response is normal. Anxiety is also normal, signaling us to take a look at the stress in our lives. Only when these symptoms—panic and anxiety—become so crippling that we can't continue our daily patterns do we have a disorder that needs to be treated.

PART ◇ II

CAUSES OF ANXIETY AND ITS DISORDERS

Biological Causes of Anxiety

PANIC ATTACKS

Panic attacks happen for a variety of reasons. Often they come from a combination of emotional and physical factors, and one sets off the other. Human beings were designed so that danger would activate the fight or flight response, which originates in the brain. Things can go awry, however—any malfunction in the brain, especially in the region of the lower brain called the locus ceruleus (which controls our emotional responses), can cause panic symptoms. Scientists have discovered that they can cause panic symptoms by stimulating this region electrically; they can also disrupt a panic attack by administering drugs or damaging the locus ceruleus.

Several different situations can set off panic symptoms in the locus cereleus. If you are extremely sensitive to carbon dioxide, you may react with panic symptoms when too much carbon dioxide is in your body. This may happen because of hyperventilation—breathing too fast and too shallow. People who are anxious tend to hyperventilate, and hyperventilating leads to a buildup of carbon dioxide circulating in the system. Carbon dioxide buildup also may happen after vigorous exercise.

There is a connection between the locus ceruleus and the quantity of neurotransmitters in that region as well. Neurotransmitters are chemicals secreted by the neurons, or brain cells, which enable the other neurons to work together. Sometimes insufficient or excessive neurotransmitters (in this case, norepinephrine and serotonin) cause the locus ceruleus to go haywire. This sets off an unnecessary panic attack. That is why certain antidepressant medications help to prevent panic attacks; they directly affect the quantity of norepinephrine and serotonin that the body produces.

ANXIETY STATES

There are several generally accepted biological causes of anxiety. The first is that people feel anxious because they have an insufficient amount of the neurotransmitter gamma aminobutyric acid, or GABA. GABA is associated with calming the brain. It actually works by inhibiting neurons that would ordinarily set off the alarm, so that high levels (or at least sufficient levels) of GABA help keep a person calm.

Also, anxiety can result from artificially stimulating the body. Drugs such as caffeine, nicotine, amphetamines, and cocaine all provoke an anxiety reaction.

One of my clients came in complaining of severe anxiety and frequent panic attacks. Dorothy worked as a data entry operator. As I probed into what kinds of stress she might be encountering at work, I learned that she was actually bored with her job. In fact, she was so bored that

she had to drink ten cups of coffee a day just to keep awake.

Ten cups of coffee!? The woman was consuming enormous amounts of caffeine! Once she decreased her coffee consumption to one cup a day, she no longer experienced anxiety.

Certain medical conditions can cause symptoms of anxiety and panic as well. In fact, more than fifty physical conditions cause anxiety. If a doctor is not careful to treat the primary medical condition, she may not be able to cure the anxiety. Endocrine disorders, such as diabetes and hypoglycemia, cause many of the same symptoms as those felt in panic attacks. Hyperthyroidism or inner ear disturbances may cause anxiety symptoms to develop as well.

A relatively harmless heart condition called mitral valve prolapse can be another trigger. Within the heart of some people, the mitral valve does not close fully after blood has passed from one chamber into another. This causes a small backflow of blood which is essentially harmless but causes some uncomfortable sensations. A person with mitral valve prolapse may feel his heart beat an extra beat or pound a little harder than usual. This usually goes away with no harm done. However, people may interpret these erratic heartbeats as the beginning of a panic attack or heart attack. If they react with alarm, their anxiety level increases, and they may indeed suffer a panic attack (although they will not suffer a heart attack).

People often suffer panic attacks after major heart surgery. They confuse the pounding heart or occasional irregular beat with a pending heart attack. Fearful of dying, they react with anxiety and set a panic attack in motion.

Other medical conditions are not causes of anxiety, but become larger problems because of anxiety. People sometimes say that asthma attacks can be brought on by anxiety. Actually, that's only partially correct—someone can't bring on an asthma attack if he or she doesn't have the condition in the first place. But anxiety can aggravate symptoms in someone who is already asthmatic.

Tourette's syndrome is another condition worsened by anxiety. Tourette's is a neurological condition that resembles obsessive compulsive disorder in that its sufferers feel compelled to do certain things to relieve their anxiety. Unfortunately, what they often feel compelled to do is curse and yell inappropriate things in public. People afflicted with Tourette's feel immeasurable pressure to do these unpleasant things. If they refrain, they only feel more anxiety. The anxiety, then, is both a byproduct of the condition and a contributor to it.

Sleep disorders are made worse by anxiety. People who are feeling anxious often don't sleep well. Some people sleepwalk; others suffer from insomnia.

Finally, certain medications can provoke anxiety as a side effect. Sometimes even the medications that are designed to treat anxiety cause anxiety. People who have become addicted to tranquilizers called benzodiazepines experience symptoms of anxiety when they stop taking the medication. In fact, as people stop using most drugs, including alcohol, they experience many symptoms of anxiety.

OBSESSIVE COMPULSIVE DISORDER

Doctors have recognized that people with obsessive compulsive disorder may have a chemical imbalance. They may suffer from unusually low levels of the neurotransmitter serotonin. Serotonin affects memory, sleep, appetite, mood, and the ability to refrain from repetitive actions. Medication known to increase levels of serotonin allows the person suffering from obsessive compulsive disorder to behave normally again.

ENVIRONMENTAL TOXINS

Finally, certain environmental toxins (insecticides, mercury, lead) can cause panic attacks. These toxins affect the brain, thus activating the alarm.

Although there is a physiological basis for many panic attacks, as well as a possible genetic component (because anxiety disorders tend to run in families), other factors, such as stress and how a person reacts to stress, play a role. We'll explore these factors in the next chapter.

Emotional Causes of Anxiety

Sometimes the way we react to stressful situations causes us to develop symptoms of anxiety.

Julie often found herself in such a situation—she preferred to have her own feelings hurt rather than hurt someone else's. One night she got a call from a guy named David, who said he was in her French class. He asked her out for the following Friday.

Julie couldn't think of who he was, but she figured it couldn't hurt to go out with him. So she said okay. Later, she called a girlfriend to ask if she remembered this guy named David.

Her girlfriend was horrified. "You know who he is! He's that guy who sits in the last row. The one who goes out with a different girl every week."

Julie tensed up. "Not the guy with girls hanging all over him."

"That's the one," her girlfriend said.

"Well, I can't go out with him," Julie said. "I can't believe I said yes. What am I going to do?"

"You'll have to call him back and tell him you forgot you had another date."

"Be serious; I can't say that. Who's going to believe I forgot I already had a date? Besides, I can't call him."

"Then I guess you're going to have to go out with him."

Julie felt a little sick. "I'll think of something," she said.

Julie tried to avoid David after that. She came to class just before the bell rang and was always the first person to leave. She stayed so busy in class that she never looked up to see if David was even there. As Friday night approached, Julie became more anxious and more ill. The butterflies in her stomach progressed into diarrhea attacks, so that by Friday afternoon Julie really was too ill to go out with David.

Did Julie have something physically wrong with her? No. Her anxiety stemmed from not knowing how to deal effectively with the stress of being asked out and not wanting to go.

A former client of mine had chronic anxiety because she worked for a boss who expected her to do the work of three people. Michelle didn't complain because she needed the job, and she was afraid he'd replace her. However, it was impossible for her to accomplish all that her boss expected. So she kept going to work although she dreaded it, and every time she was late for a deadline, she popped a tranquilizer to calm her nerves.

She didn't recognize that her symptoms of anxiety stemmed from her inability to stand up for herself or set appropriate boundaries. As long as she neglected her feelings, she felt stressed and anxious.

Stressful situations contribute to anxiety, but if people learn to deal effectively with them (as discussed in Chapter 6), they don't have to let their symptoms of anxiety turn into full-fledged anxiety disorders.

TRAUMA

Some people believe that trauma causes biological changes within the brain. Although that is certainly possible, it has not been proven conclusively. More people believe that trauma works on an emotional level to cause anxiety and panic.

Consider Shawn, whose home was wiped out by a tornado. Now, every time there's a thunderstorm, Shawn has a panic attack. The darkening sky, the roaring winds, and even the TV bulletins all remind him of the time he hid in his closet while a tornado rampaged through his neighborhood.

Shawn had been terrified that night. But because the threat was real—his life *was* in danger—the panic made sense. Now, although the panic persists, the danger is not real any more. Yes, a thunderstorm can cause a lot of damage, but most don't contain tornadoes. And Shawn, who has convinced himself that he's always in danger, suffers unnecessarily. His reaction to the traumatic event has created the anxiety and panic.

A friend of mine was bitten by a dog when she was a child. Now, Cynthia is afraid of *all* dogs, even the slow, sweet basset hound that lives next door. Being around any dog causes her to start shaking, her heart to start pounding, and her stomach to turn over. Most of the dogs she comes in contact with are friendly and obedient. However, the memory of that early attack so traumatized her that she reacts with undue anxiety every time.

PHOBIAS AND PRIMITIVE FEARS

Some people theorize that there's a reason why many of us have phobic reactions to snakes and spiders. Since some snakes and spiders are poisonous, they believe we are programmed to fear them. In primitive times, panicking and running away from snakes probably saved many lives. Unfortunately, nowadays, some of us sense that same urgency when faced with a harmless garter snake or spider. We react with panic without first assessing the danger. It's not that we've even been bitten before; we simply *feel* uneasy, and consequently, we panic. Trauma hasn't programmed us to run from these creatures; our uneasiness, which might be a holdover response from earlier times, has programmed us.

PERFECTIONIST PARENTS

Some people are more anxious than others because they've been raised by perfectionist parents. Parents who have extremely high standards of achievement may have children who make themselves ill trying to meet the expectations.

One person I know had to clean her room every night before she could go to bed. Dirty clothes had to be stashed in the hamper, and nothing could be hidden under the bed. Everything was supposed to be hung in her closet facing a certain direction. If anything was askew, her father would get her out of bed (no matter what time of night) and make her rehang the offending article of clothing. Not surprisingly, this anxious young woman went on to develop obsessive compulsive disorder.

Another young woman developed a social phobia. Her mother was extremely critical of her, finding fault with the way she looked, her grades, and her ability to make friends. Sharon's father had left the family when Sharon was very young. By the time she was a teenager, Sharon had concluded that he had left because he couldn't stand her mother's tirades. But Sharon couldn't leave; she had no place to go. Not only that, she was attached to her mother. Her self-esteem plummeted. As an awkward teenager, Sharon started feeling more and more nervous whenever she was the center of any attention. She almost fainted the day she had to give a speech in class, and she talked herself out of trying out for a softball team because too many people would be watching her.

Social phobias often develop in children raised in rigid households or by parents who are social phobics themselves.

If some children develop phobias like those of their parents, it may be because they copied the behavior they saw at home. Perhaps it has more to do with observation and imitation than with genetics. Not surprisingly, anxious parents have anxious kids.

ANTICIPATORY ANXIETY

The true panic attack comes from out of the blue. More than likely, there is a biological reason for it. But because the symptoms are so frightening, and the event is so unpredictable, the panic victim begins to fear having another one. The way she feels—nervous, sweaty palms, stomach tied in knots—is called anticipatory anxiety. In other words, she is anticipating having another panic attack at any moment, and is constantly on guard. Medication may exist to stop a panic attack from occurring, but the same medication does little to stop the buildup of anxiety.

Anticipatory anxiety comes from not knowing how to deal with the panic situation. You may talk yourself into a worse reaction, or you rely on people or substances to make you feel safe. Let's look at some of the ways we make small problems bigger.

Avoidance

Avoidance is the quickest way to convert a fear into a phobia. Whether you have been traumatized or have associated your first panic attack with a specific situation, once you start avoiding those situations, you make the fear worse. When you change your lifestyle to accommodate the fear, you have created a phobia. So, whether or not a phobia has a biological basis, emotional factors (the way we think about the event and the subsequent way we behave) maintain the phobia.

For example, I happen to dislike scorpions. I've only seen a few in my life, and fortunately most of them were in the zoo. Because I live in Oklahoma, however, I have to consider that I'll probably run into some after a while.

I don't know why I'm so frantic around scorpions. Their sting is rarely fatal, although it can make you very sick. I never considered my feelings about scorpions to be phobic. I thought they made perfect sense.

That was the case until a dear friend bought a house in the country. It's a beautiful house with enormous, sunny rooms and windows all around. It's cozy, with plants in every room and, unfortunately, a few scorpions here and there come in through the chimney.

"Don't worry," my friend said. "If you see one, just step on it."

Just step on a scorpion? I'd sooner run in front of a speeding car.

I've visited my friend twice in her new house. The first time I was very uncomfortable because I kept expecting an army of scorpions to march in from the porch. I hung out in the kitchen because the stools were high, and if I climbed up on them, my feet didn't touch the floor. I felt safer there. When she asked me to come sit with other guests in the living room, I froze. What if a scorpion was out there hiding under a plant? Can scorpions smell fear?

I cut short that first visit. The second visit was even worse. Several guests wanted to walk around the yard and down to the creek. I was paralyzed. No way was I going to walk outside when scorpions were around. So they went without me, leaving me alone in the house. I stood there feeling queasy. Then I made a run for the kitchen and climbed up on a stool. By the time they returned, I was ready to go home.

That was the last time I visited my friend. I never did encounter a scorpion, but the mere possibility haunted me. I've made myself more afraid by avoiding the place and not confronting my fear. That's what I mean when I say phobias become worse depending on what message we give ourselves. Avoidance is a strong message that some situations are too dangerous to face.

Reliance on Medication

Some people have another method of handling stressful situations. When they start feeling anxious, they pop a pill or smoke a marijuana joint. Many alcoholics started drinking because they were afraid of social encounters. Fearing the situation in which they might have a panic attack, they rely on a substance (alcohol, tranquilizers, illegal drugs) or another person to get them through the situation. If they do this often enough, they associate their relief from anxiety with taking the drug or having that particular person with them. Soon enough, they aren't able to face the situation without the drug or the person to serve as a safety net.

Reliance on safety nets works the same way as avoidance. Avoiding the source of your fears brings relief, so avoidance becomes a way of life. Likewise, turning to drugs can become a way of life because initially it brings relief from the fear. Even having a safety net (a friend to go with you when you're afraid) becomes problematic because you learn you can't handle the situation alone.

A client of mine named Lawrence had been taking three times the amount of tranquilizer prescribed by his primary-care doctor. Apparently he had been going to several doctors and getting prescriptions from all of them. Not only that, some of the doctors did not keep track of how many pills they ordered. By the time I inherited the case, Lawrence had relied so much on his tranquilizers that he had grown addicted to them and had lost faith that he could play any role in defeating anxiety himself.

Self-Talk

It's not always an event that causes the panic. More often than not, it's our self-talk (what we tell ourselves the situation means) that makes the situation worse.

One day one of my clients called me, sounding out of breath.

"I need to go to the hospital," she said, gasping for air. "And I want them to know you're my therapist, so you can tell them what medicine I should take."

"Sara, is that you?" I asked. I had never heard her so upset.

"I think something's really wrong," she continued. "I think I need to be hospitalized. I might even be having a heart attack."

"Slow down, Sara," I said. "Tell me what's going on."

"Well, I was working at the store, and all of a sudden I started to feel hot. That didn't make sense because the air conditioner was going full blast. Anyway," she said, pausing to gulp more air, "I fanned myself a little and then started feeling dizzy. I sat down and realized that my heart was pounding. It felt as if it was about to explode right there in my chest. I told my boss I was having a heart attack and going to the emergency room. Then I called you."

"It sounds as if you're having a panic attack," I said.

"But my hands feel all tingly, and I think I'm going to faint," she cried, still breathing hard.

"That's because you're hyperventilating," I said. "Do you have a paper bag handy?"

"I've got one right here," she said. "Someone once told me to breathe into a bag, and I'd stop hyperventilating."

"Well, that's right. Breathe into the bag right now."

I heard her put the bag to her face and start breathing into it. After a minute or so, her breathing became slower. She got back on the phone. "I'm breathing better," she said.

"Good," I said. "You're having a panic attack. A panic attack lasts anywhere from ten to twenty minutes; you can ride it out. If you know what's happening, you won't over-react. When you're a little calmer, come out here. We'll talk about panic attacks."

Sara agreed, and indeed she was feeling calmer by the time I saw her. Had I not known she had a history of panic attacks, I might have wondered about a heart attack, tco. Fortunately, Sara simply needed to learn how to talk herself through one of these panics. Her method had been to talk herself into a bigger panic. If a biological reason prompted the first attack, her negative self-talk kept the panic growing.

What do I mean by "self-talk"? Sara would start to feel a panic attack coming on, but instead of telling herself she could ride out the symptoms, she would think things like: "Oh, this is awful. I don't think I can handle this. What if I'm really having a heart attack this time? Can I make it to the hospital in time? Maybe I'll die this time. Maybe I won't, but I'll probably never get better. I can't live like this for another twenty years."

By the time the person finishes scaring herself, her anxiety has caused the panic attack to last longer than it would have without the negative commentary. Clearly, negative self-talk feeds anxiety and makes the symptoms worse. A better alternative is positive self-talk, which I'll talk about later in this book.

Conflict over Aggressive Impulses

Anxiety may also arise from the battle between our impulses (what we want to do) and our social conscience (what we know society will permit). This theory originated with Sigmund Freud, a renowned psychologist who thought that people grew anxious because they were afraid they might do something society considered inappropriate.

For example, Lamont lived with a stepfather—sometimes his stepfather treated him well, but more often than not, he was abusive. Lamont hated this man, but he also tried very hard to please him.

When Lamont was fifteen, he started dreaming about killing his stepfather. He would wake up in a cold sweat, incredulous that he could have dreamed up such violence. He also started worrying about sharp instruments being left around the house. He hid all the knives and buried the scissors in the bottom of a kitchen drawer. At night he hated to go to sleep for fear he would dream again.

After a few months, he started worrying that someone would break into his parents' house. He kept getting out of bed to check that all the doors were locked. Eventually, his checking took over more and more of his time.

Lamont continually struggled with his own feelings and urges. He developed an anxiety around knives because he feared he might use one. He also feared that someone would break into the house and kill his stepfather—which could be seen as a fulfillment of Lamont's wish.

IS ANXIETY BIOLOGICAL OR EMOTIONAL?

Anxiety can stem from either physical or emotional causes, or a combination of both. Even when we don't know the cause, it is wise to consider a physical cause first, because physical causes are usually easier to treat. However, it's just as likely that emotional factors are contributing to a person's anxiety, and those often take longer to treat. Changing one's reaction to stressful situations and learning to tolerate uncomfortable symptoms and to talk more positively takes a great deal of effort. That is what we'll look at later in this book. Anxiety and its disorders are treatable no matter what the cause.

Consequences of Anxiety

Terri had been listening to her parents fight for the past several days. She tried not to listen, but it was hard to ignore two people shouting at each other and slamming things around. There had been days of fighting before, but this seemed more serious, and Terri wished it would stop.

She turned off the television and went into her bedroom, closing the door behind her. Her stomach was on fire, even though she had only had soup for supper. She lay down on the bed and tried to relax. Her fiery, queasy stomach began to churn, and Terri knew she was going to be sick. She hoped her parents wouldn't hear her.

After vomiting, she wiped her face and saw droplets of blood around her mouth. Startled, she looked into the toilet and saw more blood. Her mouth tasted like iron. Should she tell her parents? Should she see a doctor?

Terri sat back on her heels on the cold bathroom floor. Something was really wrong this time. She had always had a nervous stomach, but throwing up blood was new. She clutched her stomach. It really hurt. Maybe she had cancer, she worried. She crawled back to her room, grabbed the heating pad, and tried to relax, but she still felt sick to her stomach.

Terri didn't have cancer. She had the beginnings of an ulcer, a very painful condition in which the acidic juices of the stomach start eating a hole in the stomach wall. Clearly, it's a condition that requires medical treatment. And it can be the result of constant feelings of anxiety.

PHYSICAL CONSEQUENCES

When you are anxious, your body and mind are primed for danger. When the danger is over, your body returns to normal. However, if you are chronically anxious, you feel that the danger is never over. You remain on guard. Your sympathetic nervous system is activated most of the time, and that takes a toll on your body.

In general, anxious people have a lot of physical complaints. This is mainly for two reasons. First, anxious people are tense. Muscle tension can lead to injury and chronic pain. Second, anxious people have weakened immune systems because of the ongoing physical stress of heightened alertness. Weakened immune systems make people more likely to get sick. They catch colds more easily because their bodies are less able to fight off infections.

Muscle tension leads to chronic pain. Tense people, especially those who hold in their anger, often complain that their shoulders ache. Many complain of lower-back problems that ultimately make back injuries more likely.

Anxious people feel aches and pains all over their bodies because it hurts to be so rigid all the time. Most are not even aware that they are rigid, which makes it hard to correct the problem.

Ulcers are often a result of chronic anxiety. When you're anxious, your stomach secretes more acid, and the acid can eat a hole in your stomach wall.

Irritable bowel syndrome is another anxiety-worsened disorder, but instead of the stomach, the colon is affected. People end up suffering alternating bouts of diarrhea and constipation. Irritable bowel syndrome can progress to ulcerative colitis if an ulcerated area starts to grow in the colon wall.

Bruxism develops when people grind or clench their teeth. This may happen when people are angry or afraid, especially if they're holding in these feelings. Grinding puts pounds of pressure on the teeth enamel and on the bone that surrounds the teeth. It doesn't take long for the constant wear and tear to crack a tooth, or cause the bone to break down.

Anxious people see doctors frequently. They catch more viruses, are injury-prone, and have headaches and stomach trouble with which to deal. Anxious people are not all hypochondriacs making up their illnesses. Most of the time, they really are sick; it's just that their anxiety has contributed to their illnesses.

SLEEP DISORDERS

Anxiety can also contribute to sleep disorders. People who have suffered trauma often have recurrent nightmares and night terrors. Nightmares and night terrors are both linked to anxiety, but they occur during different levels of sleep.

When you fall asleep, your body goes through four levels of sleep. Stage I is the lightest level of sleep; stage

IV is the deepest, and the most restorative to the body. After you have been in stage IV sleep for thirty minutes or so, you start to rouse from this deep state and slip back into a lighter sleep. You go up through stage III to stage II sleep. This cycle happens throughout the night. These four stages of sleep comprise NREM (non-rapid eye movement) sleep, during which the body does not typically engage in dreaming. You pass through each night drifting in and out of stages II and III, spending less and less time in stage IV.

In between the stages is another kind of sleep: REM sleep (rapid eye movement) sleep. This is when you dream. REM sleep is believed to be mentally restorative; without it, you would be edgy and irritable all the time. The REM periods get longer throughout the night. By morning you're spending much more time in REM.

Nightmares occur during REM sleep, so they frequently occur later in the sleep cycle. Nightmares are bad dreams. You wake up and usually remember the dream all too well. You're afraid and may call out to someone for comfort. You know where you are and what's going on. Nightmares happen more often to those people who are under a lot of stress, or have suffered trauma, because they are using all their energy during the day to keep thoughts of the trauma at bay. At night, when they fall asleep, their guard is down. Memories come back as bad dreams.

Night terrors happen during NREM sleep. They are not dreams; at least, not the type of dream with a storyline. When you are in stage IV sleep, you are very relaxed. If someone tried to wake you, it would be difficult. As you return to the lighter stage III sleep, you sometimes have difficulty making the transition. If you are overtired or under a lot of stress, your body resists coming out of stage IV. So you wake up. Only you don't really wake up; you only appear to be awake. You remember any scary image or thought that preceded this waking up, and you scream in virtual terror. You may thrash around or fall off the bed.

If you try to calm a person who has had a night terror, you only succeed in scaring him more because he doesn't know where he is or who you are. In the morning, he won't remember the event at all. In fact, when left alone, the person with a night terror returns to sleep.

Sleepwalking is similar to night terrors. Anxious people are more likely to sleepwalk, especially when they're older.

Finally, anxious people tend to have trouble getting to sleep. They suffer from insomnia—an inability to either fall asleep or to stay asleep. For example, people with symptoms of obsessive compulsive disorder worry a lot, and nighttime is when many do the most worrying. Obviously, dwelling on the same thought hour after hour will keep you from falling asleep and having a restful night. People who have nocturnal panic attacks may fear falling asleep. And people who have nightmares may not want to fall asleep.

Unfortunately, people who don't get adequate sleep become anxious and irritable. The anxiety that may have contributed to the sleeping problem in the first place now becomes worse—a byproduct of the sleeping problem.

PANIC AND YOUR LONG-TERM HEALTH

Panic attacks may wear you down, but they won't kill you. Panic attacks do not inevitably become heart attacks. You won't go crazy from having panic symptoms, and you won't have a stroke. In fact, you can adjust to panic symptoms, even though they can be extremely uncomfortable.

The problem isn't really with panic attacks. The anticipatory anxiety that accompanies panic attacks is much harder on your health. Panic attacks are time-limited; your body has a built-in mechanism to calm you after ten to twenty minutes. However, anticipatory anxiety lasts longer, and that can be damaging to your health. As anxiety weakens your body, it can create the climate for the onset of other diseases, like heart disease or cancer, that you may be genetically prone to. That's why treatment of anxiety is so important—and this is discussed in the next section of this book.

TREATING EVERYDAY ANXIETY

Learning to Manage Stress

Our society is a stressful one. Although many of you will not go on to develop full-fledged anxiety disorders, you *will* be subjected to stress. It's unrealistic to counsel teens to avoid stress, but you can learn ways to handle it. If you understand how stress creates anxiety, and you can effectively manage your reaction to that stress, you are less likely to develop an anxiety disorder. If you already have an anxiety disorder, you can learn more effective ways to manage the stress around you.

TEN WAYS TO MANAGE STRESS

1. Learn to recognize the signs of internal stress: the butterflies in the stomach, the pounding heart, the muscle tension. Practice relaxation techniques to calm yourself, and learn how to problem-solve so that small problems don't grow into big ones.

Relaxation techniques: Practice progressively tensing and relaxing all the muscles of your body. Start with your hand. Make a fist and clench as hard as you can. Hold that position for a few seconds so that you know how a tightened fist feels. Then release it. Relax your hand and wiggle your fingers to loosen it even more. Next tense your forearm. Try to do this without tensing your hand again. You want to isolate each body part as you tense and relax it. Hold the tense position long enough to register how it feels. Then release and shake it loose. Progress up the arm, tensing, holding, and releasing.

Move on to the other hand and arm, then to the shoulders and neck. Go on to your feet and move up your legs to the buttocks and lower back, always tensing, holding, and releasing. Do these exercises at least once a day, preferably at night, because they'll relax you and prepare you for sleep. Don't race through the exercises. Take your time. If you don't have the twenty or thirty minutes you need to do them all, spend five or ten minutes working on specific parts at a time.

Learn to control your breathing. Ordinarily, people breathe correctly, letting the abdomen expand and contract with each breath. It is called belly breathing. When stressed, a person starts to panic and breathe more quickly and more shallowly. The chest rises and falls with each breath, indicating that the lungs are not expanding sufficiently to pull in oxygen and fully expel the carbon dioxide. One of the quickest ways to relax yourself is to slow your breathing. Concentrate on the rise and fall of your abdomen. Push out your stomach, not your chest, and take the time to empty your lungs fully. If you have a tendency to hyperventilate and slowing down your breathing isn't effective, hold your breath for as long as you can. Then resume breathing more slowly.

Problem-Solving: When you have a problem, it's best to figure out exactly what the problem is and what your options are. (If you have a problem with someone else, you'll want to involve that person in formulating the options. If you practice assertive behavior, discussed in chapter 6, it is likely that you will find a solution that satisfies you both.)

In thinking up options, work to find at least three options that could solve your problem. Call them Plan A, Plan B, and Plan C. That way, if you try an option and it doesn't work out, you have two other options. People who are prepared are less overwhelmed by stressful events. The key is to be flexible, so that if one plan doesn't work, you'll have no qualms about implementing the next plan.

Let's say you're afraid that you might have trouble handling the increased academic workload in college. Instead of worrying about what might happen, it is better to plan what you'll do in the event you do have trouble with schoolwork. Plan A might be to talk with your instructors about your difficulties. Plan B might be to hire a tutor to help you. Plan C might be to drop one class and concentrate more on the ones you kept. When you know your options ahead of time, you're less likely to feel overwhelmed should problems develop.

2. Schedule "downtime" for yourself. You need relaxing time every day, not just once a week or when you've finished a major project. In downtime, you don't do anything but relax or play. Watching television while you iron is not downtime, because ironing is work. Listening to music or the sounds of nature can be relaxing if you're not also doing your homework. There's a time for homework (preferably a time when you're totally focused) and a time to relax. Downtime allows you to rest so that you do not accumulate stresses from day to day.

3. Reduce your caffeine intake—caffeine is a stimulant. It can make you feel jittery and irritable. It's supposed to increase alertness, but it also sets your nerves on edge.

Reducing caffeine means reducing the amount of caffeinated coffee and soda you drink, the amount of chocolate you eat, and the medications that contain caffeine. You'd be surprised at all the items that contain caffeine, so make it a habit to check labels before buying a product.

Nicotine is another stimulant you should avoid. Cigarettes are the primary source of nicotine. Because smoking is addictive, it's a hard habit to give up, but one well worth the effort when working to change the stress in your life.

4. Develop an exercise routine. That doesn't mean you have to work out for hours each day. Simply taking a brisk walk for thirty minutes each day is enough to keep your body in good aerobic condition. Exercising also causes the brain to release endorphins, the body's own painkillers. In fact, scientists have discovered that the one best thing you can do to guard against stress is to exercise regularly.

5. Create a calming environment around you. Play relaxing music, even if your preference is for rock or rap. You can listen to rock or rap when you want to be energized, but neither will do much to calm your nerves.

Create a "safe place" for yourself, especially if you live in an unsafe neighborhood. Everyone needs a place to go when they're stressed from the events of the day. If your home is not safe, find another place away from the danger. Some people have found special places at parks or in corners of the library. Others have created a private spot in neighboring woods or by a creek.

Not only do you want a calm environment, you want to surround yourself with calm people. That, of course, doesn't mean you can't go to wild parties. However, you are defined in part by the people with whom you choose to spend the most time. If your friends are loud and abrasive, you're likely to encounter more stress. Level-headed, low-key people, on the other hand, seem more immune to stress.

6. Learn to stand up for yourself and express your feelings. That means saying no when you feel like saying no and setting appropriate limits with other people.

A person can behave in four different ways with people. He can be *aggressive*—placing his own needs above anyone else's. He can be *passive-aggressive*—acting unintentionally in aggressive ways. He can be *submissive*—placing others' needs ahead of his own. Or he can be *assertive*—considering both his needs and the needs of others. An assertive person neither violates another's space, nor tolerates violation of his own space.

Let's say you live next door to a man who doesn't own a lid for his garbage can. Everytime he puts out his trash, either some of it blows into your yard or neighborhood dogs get into it and strew it all over your yard. You're careful about covering your own trash so that it doesn't affect anyone else. How can you get your neighbor to do the same?

If you adopt an aggressive stance, you may get up one morning, gather up all that trash in your yard, and dump it on your neighbor's lawn. Then, you may tell him that either he gets a lid for his trash or you'll see to it that both yours and his end up each week on his front steps. You may look him in the eye, maybe shake your fist at him, and lean in close to be sure he hears you right. Clearly, you are infringing on his space.

If you adopt a passive-aggressive stance, you will be too shy to confront your neighbor. But one day, you might forget to put your trash can lid on, too. You will be genuinely surprised when interested dogs sniff the food in your trash, and overturn your can into your neighbor's yard. You won't see that you may be contributing to the problem.

If you adopt a submissive stance, you may pick up your neighbor's trash each and every time it blows into your yard. You won't complain, but you'll feel annoyed. If he notices what you're doing and comments on it, you'll simply shrug and say it's no big deal. That's what neighbors are for. Meanwhile you won't look him in the eye, you'll hang your head, and you may take a step back if he comes close. In other words, you'll let him walk all over you. The only way you'll know it really bothers you is that your stomach will probably feel like it is on fire.

If you adopt an assertive stance, you'll think about the problem before you confront your neighbor. You'll pick a time when he's not busy and ask to speak to him. Then you'll explain that his trash keeps blowing into your yard because there's no lid on his trash can. While you're talking, you'll look him in the eye and speak in a level tone of voice. You'll neither stand so close that he has to take a step back nor step back yourself if he advances. You will stand your ground.

If the neighbor seems perplexed about what to do, be ready with some solutions. Suggest that he buy a cover and tie it to the garbage can so it won't fall off and blow away.

When people are assertive, they show respect both for themselves and others. Sometimes you'll want to say no. If you relent and say yes, you'll feel angry at the person for putting you in that situation and at yourself for not having the guts to say what you really felt. Unresolved anger can lead to depression and sometimes aggressive acting out. When you say no and mean it, you show respect for yourself. You also stave off any anxious feelings about the situation and the people involved.

Setting limits goes along with saying no. People, especially family members, often push you to do more than you want to do. Or they give you unsolicited advice. Set limits by determining the boundaries of your relationship. When someone oversteps that boundary, recognize it and assert yourself. People don't have the right to run your life unless you give them that right.

7. Along with asserting yourself and setting limits, learn how to express anger appropriately. It's not enough just to recognize that you're angry, although that's a starting point. People explode and hurt others when they're angry, and that's just as inappropriate as holding in anger and ending up with a tension headache.

Learning to deal with your anger begins with recognizing when you're angry, with whom you're angry, and why you're angry. Once you realize that you're angry (the clenched teeth, the churning stomach, the tension headache), consider who can change that situation, and then clarify the situation that needs to be changed.

Sometimes you feel too angry to talk to the other person. When that happens, either try to calm yourself in order to gain perspective on the situation, or wear yourself out by exercising, cleaning, or playing a sport. The goal is to give yourself time to calm down and think more clearly. Taking your anger out by hitting things (even if they aren't people) is not a good idea. Being violent doesn't calm you down; most often it increases your anger.

It's okay to tell someone you're angry. Telling someone your feelings is far better than acting them out or holding them inside. But try to look beyond the anger to the feelings underneath. These feelings are often ones of hurt, shame, or envy. Be prepared for the other person to have a different interpretation of the situation. Listen if he presents it, because you might discover that your view of the situation was not entirely accurate. Then different solutions might present themselves.

Anger itself doesn't cause more stress. The way people react to anger is the problem. If you're honest with your feelings and present them assertively (not aggressively), you stand to reduce your stress, not make it worse.

If someone else is angry with you, you can help him out and reduce your own stress by asking about it: What has angered him and how does he think the situation might be resolved.

8. Learn to manage your time better. Set priorities so that in a time crunch, you get the most important stuff done first. Set aside time to do schoolwork, time to be with friends, time to do chores or be at a job. And of course, give yourself some downtime so you won't be stressed by meeting everyone else's agenda.

Some people can accomplish more if they keep lists of things that need to be done. As they complete a task, they mark it off the list. This helps them realize how much they actually accomplish even if there are few outward signs.

Give yourself a time frame to accomplish certain things. Some things need to be done right away; others can wait until tomorrow or the next day. If you try to accomplish too much in one day, you'll probably get frustrated and give up. Set short goals, and note them when you've met them. Prioritize your tasks and do the important stuff first.

9. Get a pet if you can. Pets have been shown to decrease people's stress significantly. If you're allergic to animals or you can't have one where you live, consider

getting fish. Goldfish are inexpensive and easy to maintain. Watching fish swim around in a tank is relaxing; that's why you see so many aquariums in doctor's offices.

10. Recognize that stress is more manageable at certain times than others. When you're overtired or ill, you're more likely to be overwhelmed by events that otherwise wouldn't have seemed so monumental. When you're not coping well, delay any decisions and distract yourself until you're better able to cope. When you're worried or tired, you won't make good decisions. Distract yourself from feeling anxious and unable to cope. Promise yourself that you'll deal with the situation when you're rested. Consider that on better days, this situation might not even seem like a problem. Then attend to your health and recovery. Chronically stressful situations (such as a loved one's illness) can affect your own health. So get plenty of rest yourself, and eat well.

When you accept that stress is an inevitable part of your life, you can find ways to contain it rather than run from it. Stress was never resolved by people's pretending that it didn't exist. As you become more adept at managing stress, you will find yourself more happy, more open to new experiences, and better able to get through the inevitable bumps in life.

The Origins of Depression

When stressful situations are not managed successfully, people may react in self-defeating ways. As they start to isolate themselves and avoid the source of their fears, they become depressed as well as anxious.

Not surprisingly, depression and anxiety often go together. When people cannot control events, they may become hopeless, negative, and despairing. Donna was a shy teenager who used to avoid social interactions until she became friends with Sheila, a popular cheerleader. Sheila made it clear to her friends that Donna was to be included in all their activities, and because everyone liked Sheila, they accepted Donna as well. Donna never did overcome her discomfort in social situations, but she could tolerate the discomfort when Sheila was there with her. Sheila was her safety net.

The two girls were inseparable in high school. Sheila was voted most popular; Donna was voted most quiet.

However, when Sheila decided to go to an out-of-town college, Donna was devastated. How would she function without her friend? How could Sheila do this to her?

Donna argued and pleaded, but Sheila had her heart set on that particular school. Seeing that Sheila wouldn't change her mind, Donna applied to the school, too, but she was not accepted. What would she do?

All summer long Sheila prepared for college, and Donna worried what would happen to her at the local university. She felt that Sheila was deserting her, and she grew angry that nothing she did had any effect on her friend. She couldn't control events; her safety net would soon be gone.

The more hopeless she became, the more negative she grew. She did not have the social skills to make friends— Sheila did. Without Sheila, she would never make any new friends. By summer's end, Donna was so anxious about going to the university that she withdrew.

Living with perfectionistic, demanding parents is enough to stress many teenagers. If they try to meet the high expectations and fall short, their self-esteem suffers. They blame themselves for not measuring up instead of blaming their parents for setting unrealistic goals. Some keep trying to achieve; others give up. Those who continually fail become depressed. But it's a depression worsened by anxiety.

Hoping one day to meet these expectations, kids attune themselves to their parents, studying them for signs of how to behave. This leads to physical stress from being alert all the time and eventually to depression from not always succeeding in avoiding their parents' disappointment.

Martin's parents were both perfectionistic and abusive. They had very rigid ideas of how children should behave. Failure to meet their ideals resulted in beatings. Because Martin was the oldest, he felt responsible for his siblings' safety. He became good at tuning in to his parents' emotions, sensing when either one of them would fly off the handle. He worried when his brothers and sisters brought home poor report cards, and he tried to figure out when would be the best time to approach his parents. Because he would be the one to make the approach, he would get the first beating. By the time Martin graduated from high school, he suffered physical symptoms of anxiety: stomach problems and headaches. In addition, he had become very depressed because no matter how careful he was, he still could not control his parents' reactions.

Once he had tried to reason with his parents. His father only hit him more. Another time Martin threatened to tell school officials. His father warned that the school officials would tell the welfare people, who then would remove the kids from the home. "Then you'd all go to separate foster homes and never see each other again," his father threatened.

Martin saw no end to the violence at home. In addition to being anxious, he grew despondent. "I will never be able to control my life," he told himself.

Combatting depression and anxiety means successfully challenging cognitive distortions. Cognitive distortions are the mistaken beliefs that we have about certain events. Since stress is everywhere, the real determinant of anxiety is what we tell ourselves about our ability to manage the stress. Look back at Martin's situation. He told himself he would never be able to control events in his life. That was really a mistaken belief and what contributed to his depression. Even though he was unable to stop his father's brutal beatings, that didn't mean that his whole life would always be out of control.

Whenever you are worried about something in your life, stop and take a look at what you tell yourself during these times. Making sweeping generalizations, especially negative ones, will only compound the stressful situation. Instead, make specific comments about the event at hand or your ability today to manage the stress. Tell yourself, "Losing the race is unfortunate, but it's not the end of the world. I can always try again." Or, "Today I was too tired to play well, but I'm usually a good lacrosse player."

In fact, your ability to believe that usually you are in control relates to your success in life. Optimistic people always interpret events in their favor. Pessimistic people, on the other hand, blame themselves and put the worst possible spin on the event.

To reduce the likelihood of depression, it's important to build your self-esteem. You do that by staying involved in your world (not isolating yourself) and being productive. People who have high self-esteem see themselves as being effective. It's not necessarily that they *are* effective, only that they see themselves that way. Feeling is believing. That's where the self-talk comes in. What you say to yourself a hundred times a day is what you incorporate into your self-esteem.

Set small goals and work toward reaching them. As you see that you can meet these goals, you demonstrate effectiveness. That leads to increased self-esteem. If you set realistic goals, you won't become discouraged.

P A R T ◇ IV

TREATING ANXIETY DISORDERS

Traditional Approaches to Treating Anxiety

When the field of psychoanalysis—or "talk therapy"—began, it was believed that anxiety stemmed from wanting to do something you know is not acceptable. This conflict originated in childhood. If a person was unable to face these unacceptable urges, he or she would divert the urges into specific phobias or feel compelled to perform certain behaviors over and over.

The process of psychoanalysis was developed to probe the origins of anxiety. Modern therapists may also try to connect a person's present conflict with some unresolved conflict in the past. The emphasis is on remembering the original conflict and talking it out. The problem is that often, knowing the source of the anxiety does not necessarily stop the behavior.

Defense mechanisms serve to keep us unaware of our anxiety. All defense mechanisms are unconscious; we're not aware of them at the time we use them. A therapist's job is to bring the use of these defense mechanisms to our awareness so that we understand the source of our anxiety. At that point, we can learn how to deal with the feelings of anxiety that the original source causes. The following are all different kinds of defense mechanisms.

- *Repression*: If you repress certain bad memories, you truly forget them. You don't do this purposely; it just happens, usually when the memories are so horrible that they would cause great anxiety if remembered.
- *Regression*: A person resorts to regression when he feels overwhelmed by stress; he begins to behave in a way more suited to an earlier, less stressful time. For example, a four-year-old child gets a new baby sister. Stressed by all the attention his parents are giving the baby, he starts to act more babyish himself.
- *Sublimation*: When people have unacceptable impulses, they sometimes sublimate them by converting them into socially acceptable behaviors. For example, a sexually frustrated writer may go on to write erotic novels.
- *Rationalization*: If you've ever arrived in class without your homework and blamed it on your parents who sent you to bed early, you know what rationalization is. When you rationalize, you come up with a seemingly plausible explanation for your actions. The explanation will absolve you from blame, thereby alleviating any stress or anxiety

about a situation. The truth, if you were to admit it, would get you into trouble, thereby causing more stress.

- *Displacement*: When you take out your feelings on someone (or something) other than the cause of those feelings, that's called displacement. For example, you may get mad at your teacher about something and go home and yell at your sister. You tell yourself you're mad at your sister for squeezing the toothpaste tube in the middle, but the truth is she's done that lots of times and it never bothered you. Really you're angry with your teacher for assigning homework the night of your big game. But if you had complained about it, she would have given you even more work. Unable to face your anger at the teacher, you displace it onto your unsuspecting sister.

- *Projection*: It occurs when someone disowns certain qualities he doesn't like about himself, and starts to attribute those qualities to other people. For example, a woman who can't accept that she's a gossip may unjustly accuse her neighbor of gossiping.

- *Reaction Formation*: This defense mechanism occurs when a person can't accept his own negative feelings but makes himself believe his feelings are really the opposite. The young man who hates his father for beating him tells himself that he adores his father. When people say bad things about his father, the young man defends him. It's not a case of pretending to like his father; then his efforts would be conscious. He convinces himself that he really has such positive feelings.

The essence of traditional psychotherapy is to bring the original conflict to light, whether by examining defense mechanisms or by talking over feelings. Since the individual manages his anxiety through unconscious means, it is the therapist's job to expose the means: the defense mechanisms. By gaining insight into the source of the anxiety, the individual supposedly will stop suffering.

However, psychotherapy alone is not always sufficient to overcome panic attacks and compulsive behavior. Doctors had to start considering other approaches to combatting anxiety disorders, which I'll explain in the following chapters.

CHAPTER ◇ 9

Handling Anxiety with Cognitive and Behavioral Techniques

C ognitive and behavioral therapies involve more than just talking about the anxiety and determining its root conflict. Cognitive therapists focus on changing your thinking, and behavioral therapists focus on changing your behavior. Many therapists incorporate both approaches in a holistic attempt to treat the disorder.

Physiological reasons may explain the beginnings of panic and phobias. But what you think, and what you do about these conditions, determines how you manage them.

67

SELF-TALK AND COGNITIVE DISTORTIONS

People worsen their anxiety when their self-talk is negative. Your heart skips a beat and you think, "Oh, no. I'm having a panic attack. I'd better get out of here before it gets worse." Your teacher assigns a speech in English class, and already you start to feel sick. "I can't do this," you think. "I'll be too scared, and with everyone watching, I'll probably make a fool of myself." When you start telling yourself that you can't possibly handle a situation and that it will only get worse, your anxiety escalates.

Cognitive therapists would tell you to change your self-talk. Make it positive. Tell yourself you *can* handle this situation. If your heart skips a beat, tell yourself that happens with everyone. If it progresses to a panic attack, tell yourself you can ride out the symptoms. You *can* ride out the symptoms. A panic attack lasts only ten to twenty minutes at most. You can tolerate discomfort that long. Learn to challenge your mistaken beliefs about your situation and your ability to handle it.

People engage in many of these cognitive distortions.

- If you *overgeneralize*, you will think that something bad that happened once will always happen under the same circumstances.
- You may engage in *all or nothing thinking*—"I'm always out of control when I panic"—instead of examining each panic episode separately to find out what caused it.
- It is also common to *exaggerate*: "Everyone is looking at me."

- If you *catastrophize* when you are having a panic attack, you are predicting that the worst possible scenario is coming to pass: "I'm going crazy" or "I'm dying." You may extend this line of thinking into the future as well, and *predict* another disaster.
- The situation may get worse if you *underestimate your ability to cope* with it: "I just don't know what to do when I'm anxious. I'm not strong enough to fight it."

Most of the time people make these statements to themselves without stopping to challenge the truth of the statements. If you want to decrease your anxiety, you first have to learn to recognize your mistaken beliefs. Then you look for the fallacy in the belief and challenge it, substituting more supportive self-talk. Cognitive therapists understand that it's not so much the event that leads to anxiety as it is the way we feel about the event.

Making up and filling out a worksheet with these headings will help you become more aware of your own mistaken beliefs. Whenever you feel anxious, jot down what's going on:

- Event
- Thoughts about the event
- Cognitive distortion in that thinking
- Challenge negative self-talk by substituting more supportive statements

Let's say I've been invited out to dinner and I'm starting to panic at the thought of eating in public (a realistic fear when I was a teenager). I would fill out the worksheet this way:

Event	Thoughts about the event	Cognitive distortion in that thinking	Positive self-talk
Invitation to dinner	I won't be able to swallow.	I'm predicting the future.	I'll be nervous. If I have trouble swallowing, I just won't eat.
	Everyone will be watching me eat.	Exaggeration: Surely not everyone will spend their time watching me.	Some people might notice me, but not everyone is going to be watching me eat.
	People will think something is wrong with me.	Predicting the future again.	My date might wonder why I'm not eating much, but no one else will care.
	I might die because I can't swallow.	Catastrophizing: I may feel as if I'm dying, but nobody dies from simply not swallowing.	I might gag for a second, but I won't die.

The purpose of reframing your negative self-talk is to keep your anxiety from escalating. When something happens or you anticipate a scary event, your negative self-talk leads you to feel anxious. Once you look at the mistaken beliefs in your thinking and challenge them with more realistic, affirming statements, your anxiety should decrease. After all, it's not the event that makes you anxious; it's how you think about the event.

DEALING WITH WORRYING

Sometimes it's not helpful to spend much time countering the negative self-talk. That's true if you obsessively worry. You might spend all day filling out worksheets on your fears. In those situations, it's better to try a different approach.

You can try time limiting: indulging the urge to worry, but limiting it. First you set aside an hour (purposely choosing a long period of time) specifically in which to worry. Don't let your mind wander; keep returning to your worries.

At the end of the allotted time, stop worrying. If the thoughts come back, tell yourself you can't think about them until tomorrow.

Chances are you'll be bored before your time is up, and it will be hard to force the worrying after a while.

Another way to curb worrying is to visualize a big red stop sign every time a thought enters your head. If no one is around, shout "Stop" out loud at the same time. This behavior interrupts the thought. Although the thought may come back later, you can simply keep interrupting it. Soon enough, your mind learns to turn off that particular thought.

TECHNIQUES FOR HANDLING PANIC

Before you can learn to tolerate the sensations of a panic attack or manage the anxiety associated with your phobic situation, you have to be able to relax. Chapter 6 discussed how to practice progressive relaxation. If you practice it consistently, you will be aware when your muscles are tense and can shake them loose.

When you breathe properly, your abdomen should rise and fall, not your chest. Chest breathing results in breathing that is too shallow and is not conducive to relaxing. To make sure you're breathing correctly, lie on your back in a relaxed position. Place one hand on your belly and one hand on your chest. Inhale slowly. The hand resting on your belly should rise more than the hand resting on your chest. If that's not the case, practice exaggerating the movements when you inhale and exhale. Push your belly out as you inhale and deflate it when you exhale. Concentrate as much on exhaling as you do on inhaling. Too many people focus more on the air they're taking in and don't exhale completely. That leads to a buildup of carbon dioxide and the inevitable feelings of panic.

When you are certain of your technique, stand up and continue to breathe, pushing out your abdomen. If you exhale completely, you will be forced to breathe more slowly and deeply.

To ensure that you are breathing slowly at first, inhale to a silent count of 1-2-3. Hold that breath for two counts, then exhale just as slowly to another silent count 3-2-1. Make sure to breathe through your nose. When you breathe through your mouth, you have a natural tendency to breathe in a more shallow fashion.

Now that you know how to relax and how to breathe properly, you can incorporate these techniques when you start to feel anxious. Imagine a ladder whose rungs denote how anxious you are. Mild anxiety is on the bottom rung, progressing up through moderate anxiety to panic at the top.

Extreme panic
Panic
Strong anxiety
Moderate anxiety
Anxiety
Mild anxiety

When you are in situations that make you feel anxious, visualize that ladder and where your anxiety fits. If you register only mild anxiety, stay in the situation. If you register moderate anxiety, check your body for muscle tension. Relax the muscles and breathe more slowly. A person cannot be both anxious and relaxed at the same time.

If you find yourself hyperventilating (breathing quickly and in shallow breaths), you can do two things. Try to slow your breathing, which will be the opposite of what your body wants to do. Hold your breath as long as you can, and then resume breathing more slowly. Concentrate on the exhale as much as the inhale. If all else fails, breathe into a paper bag (never a plastic bag). Breathing in air you've exhaled will adjust the level of carbon dioxide in your body, and you will calm down.

TECHNIQUES FOR OVERCOMING PHOBIAS

Before anything else, you need to get accustomed to your internal sensations when you are distressed. *You can learn to tolerate them.* When you first notice that you are feeling anxious, pretend you're a reporter and objectively note the sensations. For example, if your heart starts to beat faster, instead of giving in to panic, simply notice the rapidly beating heart. Notice when your fingers start to feel tingly; wiggle them around. Remind yourself that your fingers feel this way because an alarm has been triggered in your body and the blood is being diverted from your fingertips to your larger muscles. Notice the butterflies in your stomach. Stay objective, and remind yourself that your stomach is reacting to the increased acidic juices.

It may help to write down on a separate sheet of paper all the physical sensations you have. If you're prone to negative self-talk, note what thoughts first come to mind when you sense distress. Challenge the distortions, and continue to observe the sensations.

Event	Physical Sensations	Self-talk

If at any point you feel yourself tensing up, concentrate on relaxing your muscles and breathing more slowly. Continue to observe the sensations as they peak and then start to subside. You can comment on the intensity of the feelings, but stay objective and don't react to the sensations. As they diminish, consider which feelings were the hardest to tolerate. Why were they hard? Did you associate them with something else? Feelings that you don't choose to fight often lose their control over you.

As you adjust to these uncomfortable sensations, keep using relaxation techniques whenever you catch yourself tensing up. Gradually you'll be able to tolerate more and more. Once you can tolerate your sensations, you're ready for the next step.

Since avoidance of any fearful situation only strengthens the phobia, a victim must face the dreaded situation. There are two ways to accomplish this. First, the person creates a hierarchy of stressful situations, much like the ladder used earlier. At the bottom, she lists the least stressful of the scenarios. She intensifies the stress as she climbs the ladder. This is called *systematic desensitization*.

If a person were afraid of spiders, she might envision her hierarchy like this.

Spider Hierarchy

Holding a spider in my hand
Sitting next to a spider
Sitting next to a spider web
Stepping on a small spider
Hearing someone say that a spider ran into your closet
Hearing someone say there's a spider in the next room
Looking at a spider through a glass barrier in a zoo
Looking at a picture of a spider in a magazine

Clearly, just looking at a spider in a magazine is the least stressful scenario, so that is where she'll begin to desensitize herself to the fear. If she's a good visualizer, she probably starts to feel anxious. At that point, she observes the anxiety and relaxes her tense muscles. She takes several calming breaths until she can think about the picture without discomfort.

Then she moves to the next level, imagining herself looking at a live spider through a glass barrier at the zoo. As that picture stirs up anxiety, she is quick to relax her muscles and take calming breaths. If she is still anxious, she visualizes another scene that calms her. Some people visualize the ocean, watching the waves crash onto the beach while listening to the sounds of seagulls flying overhead. Whatever scenario represents a safe, calming place for you will work.

When the person is calm and relaxed from visualizing her safe place, she switches back to visualizing the spider. She stays with that scenario until she can visualize it without feeling anxious. On she goes up the ladder, visualizing, feeling anxious, and teaching herself to relax.

Obviously, this is a long process. It is not completed in one sitting or even in one day. By the time she can imagine holding a spider in her hand without feeling even a twinge of anxiety, she is ready to test herself by dealing with the real situation—in this case, a spider.

Sometimes it helps to keep a chart of your desensitizing sessions. Simply record what level of the ladder you're working on, and how long it took you to master that level. If it's not easy to master, record how much time you spent for each session on that level. Some people see more progress when their attempts are recorded on paper.

Exposure involves actually experiencing the anxiety-provoking situations. The phobic person attempts this either with her therapist or another friend as a safe person. Otherwise, she may use medication to mask the symptoms of anxiety. If the person relies on a safe person or medication to get her through, she must give up the crutch as soon as possible and attempt it on her own. Most people who take medicine are surprised to discover that they relapse once they stop taking the medication.

Clearly, actual exposure is much more anxiety-provoking than imagery exposure. It won't be as easy to calm yourself, so you must learn to retreat and recover.

When the anxiety has lessened, you reexpose yourself to the situation and try to increase the time you spend in it. It doesn't matter if you have to retreat twelve times; you still must reexpose yourself until you can deal with the situation.

When you can tolerate the least stressful situation on your ladder, you move on to the next one, always exposing, calming or retreating, and reexposing. The girl with the spider phobia would actually look at a spider in a magazine, not just imagine it. She'd go to the zoo, and she'd actually touch a spider. She'd do each of the things on her list until she had conquered her fear of spiders.

HANDLING OBSESSIONS

Obsessive compulsive disorder is best treated with medication, which is discussed in the next chapter. However, behavioral techniques can be used in addition to medication. The most successful techniques with obsessive compulsive disorder are to delay responding to your urges and to distract yourself from the anxiety.

If you are a compulsive shopper, for example, you would tell yourself to wait until the next day to give in to the shopping urge. Compulsive checkers would tell themselves to wait an hour before getting up to check instead of trying to resist the urge entirely. The more you can delay, the more you get used to a little anxiety.

Just as you learned to tolerate discomfort in a panic attack, you can learn to tolerate the discomfort of a compulsion. You try to stay objective and recount how you're feeling. Then you try to focus on something else.

MEDICATIONS

Because of the physiological symptoms associated with anxiety, people seem to think that treating the symptoms will cure the disorder. Rarely does it work that way. Certain drugs will mask or temporarily treat an anxiety disorder, but they don't "cure" the anxiety. Most people need therapy to learn to manage anxiety disorders. Cognitive and behavioral therapists seem to offer the most hope, because these types of therapies focus on actively changing a person's beliefs and behaviors.

ALLOWING FOR SETBACKS

Some days you will be better able to manage your symptoms using these techniques. Other days you won't. When people have been subject to more stress than usual (a prolonged illness or a loved one's illness) or are overtired, they may not be as successful in tolerating their symptoms or challenging their cognitive distortions. When you are having trouble, recognize it as only a temporary setback. Under other circumstances, you'd be more on top of your situation. Always keep your self-talk positive.

Handling Anxiety with Medication

Anxiety disorders typically cause predictable symptoms: a rapidly beating heart, a nervous stomach, tense muscles, and blushing. Wouldn't it make sense, then, to take medication that repress these particular signs of anxiety?

Not necessarily. In addition to all the other causes of anxiety, a person can feel anxious because of certain medical conditions or because he has taken prescription or street drugs. If the actual cause is not addressed, the symptoms of anxiety are not easily managed. Thus, your first plan of attack in treating anxiety should be to see a doctor who can rule out any contributing medical problems. Be sure to tell her all the medicines you've been taking, including any illegal drugs. Certain drugs can induce panic attacks, and your doctor needs to know all the facts.

Obviously, if a medical condition is causing the symptoms, that has to be treated first. Often, the anxiety disappears as the medical condition is treated. If medications or drugs are causing the symptoms, they have to be changed or stopped altogether. Then, depending on the anxiety disorder, medication may be considered.

Years ago when I had so much trouble swallowing, my parents took me to the doctor. He initially suspected swollen tonsils, but after a complete workup, he found no physical cause. "You're having panic attacks," he finally said.

"Well, is there something I can take for it?" I asked.

He thought a moment and then scribbled something on a prescription pad. "Have your parents get this filled," he said. "It should help."

I never knew what he prescribed, but I gave the form to my parents and sat at home waiting for my relief. I had high expectations. I was going to be normal from now on when I had to eat in public. All I had to do was take this medicine (I hoped it was liquid, because I couldn't swallow pills), and I'd be calm and collected.

Only it didn't work quite that way. I took the medicine twice a day, and I gradually had less difficulty swallowing, but I didn't see the instant relief I expected. I still got nervous when I had to stand up in front of a class, and I still got a sick feeling before every major test I took. It was disappointing to discover that the medicine didn't take away my anxiety completely.

Many people think there's a magic pill out there. Medication will help relieve your symptoms, but as discussed in previous chapters, there is no single "cure."

TYPES OF MEDICATION

There are basically five types of medication used to treat anxiety disorders. The first group is the antidepressants, including the tricyclic antidepressants (called TCAs) and the MAO inhibitors (MAOIs). Both of these medications affect two neurotransmitters in the brain, norepinephrine and serotonin. MAO is a chemical in the brain that breaks down the amount of circulating norepinephrine and serotonin. An MAO inhibitor prevents this chemical from breaking down and reabsorbing these two neurotransmitters.

Another group of antidepressants are the Selective Serotonin Reuptake Inhibitors (SSRIs). These medications specifically target the neurotransmitter serotonin and keep the neurons from reabsorbing it so quickly.

A third type of medication used is the benzodiazepines, the minor tranquilizers and the more sedating drugs. This is the group most often preferred and abused by people because the relief is the quickest.

A fourth type of medication is the beta-blockers. These drugs are often used to treat high blood pressure and manage the symptoms associated with anxiety: pounding heart, blushing, and sweating.

The fifth type of medication used is the antihistamines, which correct inner ear disturbances that may produce anxiety symptoms.

Your doctor will determine when medication is appropriate and which type would work best to handle your symptoms. In any case, a combination of medication and cognitive/behavioral therapy provides the most lasting relief from anxiety.

TREATING PANIC DISORDER

Panic disorder, during which panic attacks arise seemingly out of the blue, responds best to low doses of the TCAs. These medications: imipramine (Tofranil), desipramine (Norpramin), amitriptyline (Elavil), and trazodone (Desyrel) are all effective in curbing panic attacks, although they do not affect the anticipatory anxiety that often accompanies panic disorder.

People treated with TCAS also need to practice cognitive and behavioral techniques to reduce their anticipatory anxiety. Once they learn that their panic attacks are under control, they won't have to live in fear that the attacks will resurface in uncomfortable situations. That involves challenging this cognitive distortion (I'm so nervous I'm going to have a panic attack!) and practicing positive self-talk and relaxation techniques.

TCAS target the part of the brain, the locus ceruleus, that actually causes panic attacks. TCAS actually prevent panic attacks from occurring, so medication should be considered first in treating this disorder. Cognitive and behavioral strategies also aid treatment.

TCAS are not addictive; people need not worry about long-term use of this medication. They will not build up a tolerance to them. Unfortunately, TCAS have some unpleasant side effects, such as dry mouth, and they take up to four weeks to work.

If a person is unable to find relief with the TCAS, a doctor might prescribe the MAOIS. These often work quite well, but they can lead to a dangerous rise in blood pressure if the person also eats cheese or certain meats, or drinks wine. In fact, when taking MAOIS, you have to follow a very strict diet and avoid nasal decongestants and other medications that don't combine well with MAOIS. Warnings of drug interactions are always included on packages. Phenelzine (Nardil) is the most commonly prescribed MAOI.

When people object to the side effects of TCAS and the dietary requirements of MAOIS, a doctor might try an SSRI instead. These newer antidepressants have fewer side effects, although in some people they may cause agitation.

No one really understands why antidepressants block panic attacks, but they do. If anxiety is complicated by depression, a doctor might prescribe a higher dosage of these antidepressants, as panic disorder responds to low doses.

The benzodiazepines are used to manage the signs of anticipatory anxiety, but they are ineffective in preventing panic attacks. Alprazolam (Xanax) is commonly prescribed these days on a short-term basis. It provides rapid relief (within twenty minutes) that lasts approximately four hours. Combined with TCAs, benzodiazepines would be entirely effective in controlling panic and anticipatory anxiety. The drawback is that benzodiazepines are highly addictive.

SIMPLE PHOBIAS

When people are afraid of animals, snakes, heights, or water, imipramine can be used to take care of the panic attacks that accompany the phobias. However, it does nothing about the avoidance behavior that maintains the fears. Some people require benzodiazepines in order to practice the behavioral techniques used to desensitize phobics. The short-acting benzodiazepines bring quick relief and a blunting of feelings (meaning that you won't sense your distress as acutely), which allows many people to come in contact with the situations they fear. However, the use of benzodiazepines has to be a temporary measure and a prelude to desensitizing oneself without medication.

If a doctor determines that your phobia is a result of an inner ear dysfunction, he'll probably prescribe antihistamines and decongestants. Commonly used are Antivert and Sudafed. However, don't try self-medicating just because some of these medications are available over the counter. Only a doctor trained in recognizing and treating inner ear dysfunction should prescribe medicine for this disorder.

People who are afraid of public exposure or humiliation often benefit from beta blockers. These medications (specifically, propranolol or Inderal, and clonidine or Catapres) control the manifestations of anxiety: the pounding heart, the blushing cheeks, the sweaty brow. Many people are able to handle potentially scary public encounters only when they take medication first. Without the physical signs of distress to react to, they do not develop further symptoms.

OBSESSIVE COMPULSIVE DISORDER

With this disorder, medication is the first line of defense. The antidepressant clomipramine (Anafranil) is the treatment of choice and has been used for years in Europe. However, it has some unpleasant side effects, including weight gain, so many doctors prefer to prescribe the SSRIS. The antidepressants that target serotonin seem to have the best potential for disrupting the compulsive behavior and obsessive thoughts of this disorder. Fluoxetine (Prozac), sertraline (Zoloft), paroxetine (Paxil), and more recently Luvox are all important in controlling this disorder.

Sometimes medication alone does not control all the symptoms, and behavioral strategies are needed to supplement the medicine. Delaying and distracting techniques are helpful in providing some measure of control over this disorder, but in general, it responds best to medication. Whatever the specific cause of obsessive compulsive disorder, it appears to be chemical in nature.

GENERALIZED ANXIETY

Although there are drawbacks to using benzodiazepines, some people simply have too much anxiety to learn to use behavioral techniques without first calming their nerves with benzodiazepines. The TCAS and MAOIS are not helpful with generalized anxiety because they specifically work to prevent panic attacks.

Benzodiazepines are prescribed for short-term or sporadic use. When a person has become dependent on them, he will have to taper his dose very slowly under a doctor's supervision to come off of them.

PROBLEMS WITH USING MEDICATION

Medications do provide quick and occasionally lasting relief, but there are drawbacks to reliance on them. As mentioned earlier, medications, especially benzodiazepines, are not particularly helpful with overcoming phobias.

Using drugs to address your anxiety teaches you to rely on something other than yourself. I had to learn to control my physical symptoms of anxiety when I ate in public. If my doctor had found that magic pill, I would never have realized that I could manage the anxiety by using cognitive and behavioral techniques. I would have been like Dumbo in the Disney movie, believing I could fly because I was holding a magic feather. While medications are useful in treating chemical disturbances (and admittedly some disorders are caused by chemical disturbances), they have no effect on attitudes or ability to handle stress. Those are best learned by practicing cognitive and behavioral strategies to reduce stress.

When You Need Professional Help

A t what point do you consider professional help? The answer isn't really clear-cut. Some people can tolerate more anxiety than others before they feel compelled to do something about it; some people don't mind professional help; others believe they should be strong enough to handle their problems themselves. The bottom line is this: When anxiety so interferes with your life that you're not able to carry on your normal activities on a daily basis, you need professional help.

People who break a leg or have appendicitis have no qualms about going to a doctor. Why should mental anguish be any different? You wouldn't expect a person to be strong enough to heal a broken leg on his own, would you? But typically, people think a person should be able to manage his anxiety.

If you suffer disabling panic attacks or obsessions, if you're unable to avoid your phobias or do anything about them, you need professional help. Professional help is not always a psychiatrist, either. Often, anxiety disorders are the result of chemical changes in your brain or medical conditions. It makes sense to have your primary-care physician check you out before thinking the trouble is "all in your head."

Communities are now observing Anxiety Screening Day. Various mental health agencies and counseling offices conduct free assessments for people who believe they suffer from anxiety. Unfortunately, people can demonstrate anxiety symptoms without having a psychological disorder. Some mental health practitioners assume that if you come in for treatment, you probably have a psychological disorder. Most people could benefit from seeing their primary-care doctor first. If nothing physical shows up to account for your anxiety, then you would look for psychological explanations.

PRIMARY-CARE DOCTORS

The first place to start looking for help is your primary-care doctor—your regular family doctor who generalizes in medicine. He will do a workup to determine the cause of your anxiety. That may entail blood work, X rays, and a thorough physical exam. He will ask about your family history as well, so know ahead of time if any aunts, uncles, grandparents, or siblings have certain disorders. If the doctor rules out physical problems, he may refer you to a mental health professional for treatment.

FINDING A THERAPIST

Several considerations should come to mind when you're thinking about finding a good therapist. You want to use someone who is covered by your medical insurance; you want to use someone with whom you feel compatible; and you certainly want to use someone who is competent. So how do you go about finding the right therapist?

First of all, if you or your parents have insurance to pay for mental health treatment, you need to find out which therapists are covered. Some insurance groups have specific contracts with individuals or agencies to provide services, and those people will be your only choices. If you have no insurance and a limited ability to pay, you'll probably have to go to a community mental health center. Mental health centers charge people based on their ability to pay. They use a sliding-scale fee to determine how much, if anything, services will cost.

Finding a therapist with whom you'll work well is harder to do ahead of time. Word of mouth is nice, but the therapist your friend uses may not be to your liking. Therapists have different personalities and approaches, and you can't tell what they are until you see them. Furthermore, you can't judge a person by his or her appearance.

The only way to be satisfied with a therapist is to assess how you feel around him or her. If you are still uncomfortable after five or six sessions, you might discuss finding someone else. Bear in mind, however, that therapy itself is not a pleasant and anxiety-free process. After all, you're trying to learn some techniques that take time and effort to acquire; you're also taking a look at some problems (traumatic events or situations) that will stir up uncomfortable feelings.

Above all, you want to find a therapist who is competent. Many insurance companies require you to see someone who is licensed, which means that he or she has passed a national exam and had a certain number of years of education and supervision.

Additionally, you need to find someone who understands all the treatments available for anxiety disorders—the cognitive and behavioral components, as well as the appropriate medication for your particular disorder. Some people specialize in treating anxiety and advertise themselves that way; others are simply knowledgeable in the area from experience.

TYPES OF THERAPISTS

When choosing a therapist, you should consider psychiatrists, psychologists, clinical social workers, licensed professional counselors or outpatient therapists (the usual designation at a mental health center), and clinical nurses.

Psychiatrists are the only ones who are also medical doctors. They are therefore the only ones who can prescribe medication. However, a visit to a psychiatrist's office is costly (more than $100 per twenty-minute visit), and some are only comfortable discussing and prescribing medication. If an undiagnosed medical condition is clouding the picture, the psychiatrist might be quicker at spotting it, but you do not necessarily have to see a psychiatrist to get quality care. Often psychologists and social workers refer their clients who need medication to psychiatrists with whom they have a working relationship.

Psychologists have a Ph.D. or a Psy.D. degree. They are not medical doctors, but have undergone a course of study for several years and have had experience in a clinical setting. They are often knowledgeable about testing and can both administer and assess psychological tests if any are needed to diagnose your disorder.

Clinical social workers may have either an M.S.W. degree or a doctorate in social work. They are usually very well trained, providing most of the services to clients in mental health settings. They are also slightly less costly than psychologists and definitely less expensive than psychiatrists. Their sessions usually run about $80 an hour.

Psychiatric nurses, or clinical nurses, are also good choices because of their familiarity with medications and physical disorders. They are registered nurses with advanced degrees (usually a master's degree) in counseling.

Is one category better than another? Not necessarily. It really comes down to the individual's level of competence and personality. Just because your insurance requires that you see a psychologist, for example, that doesn't mean that clinical social workers or clinical nurses are not as competent. Also, some companies prefer social workers over psychologists because they charge less for services.

ETHICAL BEHAVIOR

No matter what the profession, all therapists are bound by the same set of ethics. They are not allowed to have a physical relationship with you (even if you'd be receptive to one) and are not allowed to threaten or coerce you. If that ever happens, you have the right to stop services immediately and report them to their licensing boards. If you're afraid to report them yourself, tell your story to another reputable therapist.

Likewise, therapists should not spend your time discussing their problems (unless there's some connection) or asking you to do them favors. Therapy is a business relationship. The therapist provides the services, and you pay for them. Becoming friends with your therapist so that you can do things together alters that business relationship. It's not ethical.

LENGTH OF TREATMENT

How long will you be in treatment? Insurance companies often specify how many sessions they will pay for, based on the diagnosis. Beyond that, your therapist will recommend that you stay in treatment as long as it takes to gain mastery over your disorder. Some people function well seeing the doctor once every three months for medication. Others need to see their therapist more often to practice behavioral techniques to manage their anxiety. No longer is it a requirement that a person see his therapist every week for the rest of his life. When you can handle your anxiety without professional help, you're done with treatment. That's not necessarily left up to the therapist to decide.

SUPPORT GROUPS

Support groups are particularly helpful for people with anxiety disorders. Participants learn how others with anxiety have managed their disorders, and because the setting is public, they learn how to improve their social skills at the same time. Support groups may or may not be run by professionals. Sometimes former clients start a group to get together with others like themselves. They share advice on what strategies have worked for them, and which therapists were most helpful. Most of these groups are not closed, meaning that people can join and drop out as they choose. It's helpful to have a professional therapist guide you in your recovery, but there's a lot to be said for having allies who share your symptoms.

TRAUMA—RECOGNIZING THE STEPS TO HEALING

If you have been severely traumatized, you need professional help. It's not enough simply to escape the traumatic situation, because the memory of the trauma remains to haunt you and can create feelings of anxiety or panic. Healing comes from mastering three steps. First, you have to remember what happened and reexperience the impact. For most people, that does not feel safe, which is why they need to do their remembering with a therapist.

The second step is dealing with those feelings and grieving for your losses. The most prevalent feelings that surface from sexual abuse survivors are shame and guilt. These feelings are harder to accept than hurt and anger because it means that people feel responsible for being abused. Therapy is helpful in dispelling the idea that the victim had any control over his or her situation. Of course, accepting how powerless you once were is a scary proposition. The feeling stage of treatment lasts a long time.

The final step is to move on and know how to protect yourself in the future. Whatever it takes to create a feeling of safety is what the survivor and therapist address. Working through these issues is a long process, but it's necessary for achieving peace.

HOSPITALIZATION

Sometimes anxiety is so disabling that it requires hospitalization. Inpatient treatment is considered only when a person is thought to be a danger to himself or others, or is unable to meet his everyday needs. Some people become suicidal when they panic. They fear that no one will ever be able to help them, so they try to take their own lives. If you have these feelings, you will need to be in a hospital where staff can keep you safe until your panic has been treated.

Sometimes people are hospitalized so that they can have more extensive testing. When physical disorders are suspected of causing anxiety, patients may be hospitalized while the physical cause is being diagnosed. More often than not, these patients are hospitalized in a general hospital setting.

When people can no longer attend to their everyday needs (go to work, buy groceries, take care of their families) because of extreme anxiety, they may need to be hospitalized either in the psychiatric wing of a general hospital or in a psychiatric hospital. Hospitalization is always a last resort, and the stays are as short as possible. For many anxiety sufferers, hospitalization comes as a relief. Hospital staff involve the patient's family as much as possible, with the goal of sending the patient home at the first opportunity.

Needing professional help is not a crime. Anxiety disorders are complicated problems, and sometimes medication is needed. Some people can learn all they need to know to manage their anxiety by reading various books like this one. Others need to talk with therapists to learn how to practice the strategies correctly. However you deal with your anxiety is okay as long as your symptoms are well under control. We all experience anxiety from time to time, but there's no reason to be incapacitated by it for long.

Appendix: Medications Used in Treating Anxiety Disorders

Generic Name	Brand Name
Antidepressants (TCAs and MAOIs)	
amitriptyline	Elavil
clomipramine	Anafranil
desipramine	Norpramin
doxepin	Sinequan
imipramine	Tofranil
nortriptyline	Pamelor
trazodone	Desyrel
phenelzine	Nardil
tranylcypromine	Parnate
Antidepressants (SSRIs)	
fluoxetine	Prozac
sertraline	Zoloft
paroxetine	Paxil
	Luvox
Benzodiazepines	
alprazolam	Xanax
chlordiazepoxide	Librium
clonazepam	Klonopin

diazepam	Valium
lorazepam	Ativan
temazepam	Restoril
triazolam	Halcion

Other medications
(beta-blockers
and antihistamines)

Antivert
Marezine
Dramamine
Benadryl
Atarax
Ritalin
Dexedrine
Sudafed
Dimetapp

Glossary

adrenaline   Hormone secreted by the adrenal glands that raises the blood pressure, causing the heart to pound and the senses to become alerted to the possibility of danger.

aggressive   Disposed to dominate without regard for the feelings of others.

agoraphobia   Abnormal fear of being in open or public places.

all or nothing thinking   Tendency to assume the worst in a situation without first examining the basis of its threat.

anticipatory anxiety   Tendency to make a situation worse by imagining a bad outcome in advance.

antidepressant   Medication designed to reduce mental depression.

antihistamine   Medication to lessen allergic reactions.

assertiveness   Acting with confidence without infringing on the rights of others.

behavioral reaction   The actions a person takes in response to a perceived threat.

benzodiazepines   Group of drugs, including the tranquilizers, prescribed to alleviate panic attacks.

beta-blocker   Medication to relieve high blood pressure and the symptoms of an anxiety disorder.

bruxism   Grinding of the teeth, especially during stress.

catastrophize   To predict disaster when having a panic attack.

cognitive distortion   Mistaken beliefs about events that cause stress; conviction that the worst will occur as a result.

cognitive reaction   Way of thinking about anxiety that may actually increase the severity of anxiety attacks.

defense mechanism   Unconscious mental approach to a problem to try to solve it.

displacement   Transfer of anger against a powerful person to another person who poses no threat.

downtime   Period specifically set aside for relaxation, without the need for accomplishing any task.

exposure   Act of putting oneself in actual contact with the object of a phobia.

hypochondriac   Person suffering from depression and complaining of various, often imaginary, physical ailments.

insomnia   Inability to fall asleep or stay asleep; may have a physical or psychological basis.

irritable bowel syndrome   Disorder of the colon involving alternate diarrhea and constipation; made worse by anxiety.

mitral valve prolapse   Nondangerous heart condition that causes a backflow of blood; the accompanying pounding of the heart may cause anxiety leading to a panic attack.

obsessive compulsive disorder   Mental disorder involving the need to repeat a behavior, such as handwashing.

overgeneralize   To believe that a stressful event will always occur under the same conditions.

passive-aggressive   Unconsciously disposed to act in a demanding way, without regard for the feelings of pothers.

phobia   Strong fear of an object or a situation, long-lasting, and sometimes unnecessary. Simple phobia is fear of a specific thing. Social phobia is a fear of embarrassing oneself in public.

physiological   Pertaining to physical symptoms of the body.

predict   To expect further disasters when in a state of panic anxiety.

rationalization   Application of plausible and creditable motives to questionable behavior.

reaction formation Defense mechanism by which one credits oneself with good motives when they are actually negative.

regression Defense mechanism in which one reverts to an earlier, less stressful, time of life.

repression Defense mechanism in which one unconsciously forgets traumatic events.

stimulant Substance that causes a temporary increase of the function of the body or a part of the body.

sublimation Defense mechanism in which one disguises unacceptable impulses by changing them to socially acceptable behaviors.

submissive Having a tendency to give in to others, putting their concerns ahead of your own.

systematic desensitization Gradual elimination of obsessive fears by making contact with the feared object.

Tourette's syndrome Condition in which a person has an uncontrollable urge to scream, shout, and use obscene language.

ulcer Open sore in the stomach wall caused by excess production of stomach acids, sometimes as a result of stressful conditions.

Where to Go for Help

HOTLINES

Anxiety/Panic
800-647-2642

Depression
800-969-6642; 800-243-2525

Emotions Anonymous
612-647-9712

National Foundation for Depressive Illness
800-248-4344

National Mental Health
800-468-1515 (24 hr.)

Youth Crisis Hotline
800-448-4663

INFORMATION/REFERRALS

Anxiety Disorders Association of America
Suite 513
6000 Executive Boulevard
Rockville, MD 20852
301-231-9350

National Anxiety Foundation
3135 Custer Drive
Lexington, KY 40517-4001

Obsessive Compulsive Foundation
P.O. Box 70
Milford, CT 06460
203-878-5669

Phobics Anonymous
P.O. Box 1180
Palm Springs, CA 92263
619-322-COPE

WEB SITES

Anxiety Disorders
http:www.nimh.nih.gov/publicat.anxiety.htm

Noodles' Panic-Anxiety Page
http:www.algy.com/anxiety/panic.html

For Further Reading

Benson, Herbert, and Eileen Stuart. *The Wellness Book*. New York: Simon & Schuster, 1992.

Berent, Jonathan. *Beyond Shyness*. New York: Simon & Schuster, 1993.

Bilodeau, Lorraine. *The Anger Workbook*. Center City, MN: Hazelden Educational Materials, 1992.

Bourne, Edmund. *The Anxiety and Phobia Workbook*. Oakland, CA: New Harbinger Publications, Inc., 1995.

Carlton, Jean. *Panic No More*. Tulsa: Stonehorse Press, 1994.

Carter, Les, and Frank Minirth. *The Anger Workbook*. Nashville: Thomas Nelson, 1993.

Davis, Martha, Elizabeth Robbins Eshelman, and Matthew McKay. *The Relaxation and Stress Reduction Workbook*. Oakland, CA: New Harbinger Publications, Inc., 1995.

Lark, Susan. *Anxiety and Stress*. Berkeley, CA: Celestial Arts, 1996.

Simpson, Carolyn, and Dwain Simpson. *Coping with Post-Traumatic Stress Disorder*. New York: Rosen Publishing Group, 1997.

Zuercher-White, Elke. *An End to Panic*. Oakland, CA: New Harbinger Publications, Inc., 1995.

Index